You Can Have

Abundant Life

by Jerry Savelle

Unless otherwise indicated, all
Scripture quotations are taken from
the *King James Version* of the Bible.

14th Printing

You Can Have Abundant Life
ISBN 0-89274-327-1
Copyright © 1984 by Jerry Savelle
P. O. Box 748
Crowley, TX 76036

Printed in the United States of America.

How To Obtain The Abundant Life: Becoming A Child Of God

I have some questions for you. Do you have *assurance* in your heart of salvation after death? If you were to die, are you *certain* that you would go to heaven? Do you KNOW where you stand with God?

Unless you have received Jesus into your heart as the Lord of your life, then you are separated from God. It was never God's will or intention to be separated from the man He created, and it was not so in the beginning. God's purpose for the creation of man was so that He could have fellowship with that man. The Bible tells us in Genesis 1:26 that God said, *Let us make man in our image, after our likeness.* God longed for fellowship with someone who was like Himself.

Man, however, sinned in the Garden of Eden, and spiritual death entered into his heart. Adam and Eve disobeyed God even

3

though God had told them in Genesis 2:17 that if they did, *they would surely die*. Sin separates man from God. First came spiritual death (separation from God), followed by the death of their bodies. Spiritual death entered the hearts of Adam and Eve, and it became the nature of every man born into the world thereafter. The Bible tells us this in Galatians 3:22, *But the scripture hath concluded ALL under sin*. Man, lost in spiritual death and separated from God by sin (disobedience), could no longer fellowship with God.

But I have some "Good News" for you (that's what the word gospel means — "Good News"). God has not left man in this lost condition. He has made the way for mankind to come back into right standing and fellowship with Him; He has made a way to remove the sin and separation. John 3:16 tells us what God has done: *For God so loved the world, that he gave his only begotten Son, that whosoever believeth in him should not perish, but have everlasting life*. That is "Good

News", isn't it? God loved mankind so much and so desired man's fellowship that He sent Jesus to the cross to die and pay the price for the sin that had separated God from His creation. God is love. LOVE was the reason that God sent Jesus to earth as a man. LOVE put Jesus on the cross to die for your sins.

But God is also a God of justice. Man had sinned and justice demanded punishment. II Corinthians 5:21 reveals how the demands of justice were met: *For he made him (Jesus) to be sin for us, who knew no sin; that we might be made the righteousness of God in him.* On the cross, the sins of mankind were laid upon Jesus. Jesus suffered the consequences for every one of your sins personally. He bore the punishment for your sins in your place. He was your substitute. The "Good News" is that God is no longer holding your sins and trespasses against you. The demands of justice have been met. Jesus met those demands for every man.

Now what is left to be done? The work on the cross has to be *received* by man. Salvation is real and it is available; but in order for it to be effective in a man's life, it must be received. In John 14:6 Jesus said, *I am the way, the truth, and the life: no man cometh unto the Father, but by me.* There is only one way to have salvation and eternal life with God in heaven. It comes through *receiving* Jesus as Lord and Savior. Acts 4:12 says, *Neither is there salvation in any other: for there is none other name under heaven given among men, whereby we must be saved.* You cannot come to God or find salvation in any other name. Buddha can't save you. Mohammed can't save you. None of the doctrines or philosophies of man can give you eternal life. This comes only through receiving Jesus as your Lord.

Salvation, therefore, is available to every man, but it is not automatic. 2 Peter 3:9 says that God is not willing that *any* should perish, but He will not violate a man's will. Man has the right of choice. He can *choose* to make Jesus his Lord and receive eternal life, or he can *choose* to remain in darkness. Man's *will* — that is the freedom of choice to determine the **course** of his life — determines the final outcome.

What must be done to receive eternal life? How does one become a Christian? The Bible says in John 3:3, *Verily, verily, I say unto thee, Except a man be **born again,** he cannot see the kingdom of God.* Through Adam's sin, spiritual death entered into man's nature. Now in order for man to come back into fellowship with God, he must be "born again" from spiritual death unto life.

Nicodemus did not understand Jesus when He said that man had to be "born again" to see the kingdom of God. He asked, *How can a man be born when he is old? can he enter the second time into his mother's womb, and be born?* Jesus explained that He was not talking of a physical rebirth, but a rebirth of the spir-

7

it. In the "born again" experience, the spirit of the man receiving Jesus as his Lord is recreated in the very likeness and image of God. In his spirit, he becomes a new man.

You see, you are a three-part being. You are a spirit, you have a soul (the mind, will, intellect, and emotions), and you live in a body. It is the *spirit* of man that is recreated in the new birth.

Let's closely examine how this works. 1 Peter 1:23 tells us *how* the new birth occurs: *Being born again, not of corruptible seed, but of incorruptible, **by the word of God, which liveth and abideth** for ever.* God's Word is the seed which will bring about the new birth. Without the Word, without this seed, the new birth cannot take place. It is *by the Word of God* that you can be born again and become a partaker of the divine nature of God.

How can this be? Mary, the mother of Jesus,

asked that same question of the angel that God sent to tell her of the forthcoming birth of Jesus. In Luke 1:34, after the angel had told her that she would be the mother of the Son of God, she asked, *How shall this be?* In verse 35 the angel replied, *The Holy Ghost shall come upon thee, and the power of the Highest shall overshadow thee: therefore also that holy thing which shall be born of thee shall be called the Son of God.* In verse 38 Mary replied, *Be it unto me according to thy word.*

So it is with the rebirth of the spirit of a man. The Holy Ghost shall come upon you, and the power of God shall overshadow you. As you receive the divine seed (the Word of God) into your spirit, a miracle takes place. The spiritual death that entered man's heart at the time of Adam's disobedience is driven out by the power of God, and your spirit is recreated in God's image. His life enters your spirit as you receive His Word. God does no less a miracle in the rebirth of the human spirit than He did at the virgin birth of Jesus.

When you receive the Word of God, something very powerful happens. Colossians 1:13 tells us that when one is born again, he is delivered from the power of darkness (sin), and translated into the kingdom of his dear Son (eternal life). In other words, Satan loses the right to control your life from that point on because BY YOUR CHOICE you are no longer a subject of his kingdom. 2 Corinthians 4:4 tells us that Satan is the god (ruler) of this world. Because of your decision to receive Jesus as your Lord, you are set free from his authority and received into the kingdom of God. Satan's dominion of your life legally comes to an end at this time. He is no longer your god. You have a new nature and a new Father. 2 Corinthians 5:17 tells us this: *Therefore if any man be in Christ, he is a **new creature**: old things are passed away; behold, all things are become new.* There is a whole new way of life for you to learn about. Life in the kingdom of God is very different from life in this world. Now, through knowledge of God's Word, you can learn to walk in that which Jesus has provided for you.

Remember, 1 Peter 1:23 says that you are born again by the Word of God. What is the Word of God for one seeking salvation? Romans 10:9-10 is God's Word that brings new life to the spirit of a man: *If thou shalt confess with thy mouth the Lord Jesus, and shalt believe in thine heart that God hath raised him from the dead, thou shalt be saved. For with the **heart** man believeth unto righteousness; and with the **mouth** confession is made unto salvation.* To be born again into the kingdom of God, believe in your heart that Jesus was God's Son, that He died for your sins on the cross, and God has raised Him from the dead. Then confess this with your mouth because you believe it. Remember, in Luke the first chapter, Mary *believed* the Word that the angel of God brought to her, and as she received it, she said,

11

Be it unto me according to thy word. As you believe in your heart that Jesus was God's Son and is raised from the dead and make this confession with your mouth, it will be done unto YOU according to the Word of God. YOU WILL BE BORN AGAIN! You will be saved! Eternal life will be yours.

Now Satan doesn't want you to believe that. But Jesus said in John 6:37, *Him that cometh to me I will in no wise cast out.* No matter what you've done, Jesus paid the price for that sin and God the Father will receive you today. Once you come to God, the past is wiped out forever. Hebrews 8:12 says, *For I will be merciful to their unrighteousness, and their sins and their iniquities will I remember no more.* Glory to God! You can stand before God cleansed of every sin.

Satan can't stop you from being born again. Remember, you have the right of *choice.* If you determine in your heart to receive Jesus, no devil in hell can stop you.

Now the only thing left for Satan to do is to try to make you doubt your salvation once you've received Jesus as your Lord. One day you might get up and not "feel" so good. You may not "feel" saved. You may not "look" much like a child of God right at that moment either. But your "feelings" or how you "look" have nothing to do with your salvation. God never changes. He is the same yesterday, today, and forever (Hebrews 13:8). His *Word* is true and it never changes. Your "feelings" may change, but God's Word won't. His Word in your heart is what is true. So doubts and the temptation to fear may come, but just keep right on walking with God and believing in Him. The Word of God says that Jesus will *never* leave you nor forsake you (Hebrews 13:5). *Believe* on His Word. Once you make Jesus your Lord, you are a part of the family of God *forever*.

Is there any reason that you can't make Jesus the Lord of your life right now? Please pray this prayer out loud with me. Pray with a sincere and trusting heart, and you will be born again.

Dear God in Heaven,
I come to you in the Name of Jesus to receive salvation and eternal life. I believe that Jesus was Your Son. I believe that He died on the cross for my sins and that You raised Him from the dead. I receive Jesus now into my heart and make Him the Lord of my life. Jesus, come into my heart. I welcome You as my Lord and Savior.
Father, I believe Your Word that says I am *now* saved.
I confess with my mouth that I am saved and born again.
I am *now* a child of God.

Now begin to praise God for your salvation and thank Him that you have been born again. You have been received into the kingdom of God. 1 John 3:2 says, *Beloved, NOW we are the sons of God.* As you gain knowledge of God's Word and the principles of this new kingdom, you can learn to walk in the inheritance you have as a child of God.

How To Be Filled With
The Holy Spirit

Before Jesus died on the cross, He told His disciples that He would be leaving them. He went on to explain that they would not be left alone. In John 14:16-17 Jesus said, *And I will pray the Father, and he shall give you another Comforter, that he may abide with you for ever; Even the Spirit of truth; whom the world cannot receive, because it seeth him not, neither knoweth him: but ye know him; for he dwelleth **with you,** and shall be in you.*

When you received Jesus as the Lord of your life, you were born again *of* the Spirit of God. Your sins were forgiven and you became a child of God. There is a difference, however, in being born *of* the Spirit and being *filled with* the Spirit. John 14:17 clearly states that the world (the unbeliever separated from God by sin) cannot receive the Holy Spirit. We see by this that there are two distinct and separate operations of the Spirit in the heart of man. The first is the re-creation of the human spirit in the new birth, and the second is the infilling (or indwelling) of the Spirit after salvation. ONLY PEOPLE WHO ARE BORN AGAIN BY THE SPIRIT OF GOD CAN BE FILLED WITH THE HOLY SPIRIT. The world (those outside of Christ) are not eligible for this experience.

The eighth chapter of Acts illustrates this clearly:

Verse 5 — *Then Philip went down to the city of Samaria, and preached Christ unto them.* Philip preached the message of salvation to the Samaritans.

Verse 12 — *But when they believed Philip preaching the things concerning the kingdom of God, and the name of Jesus Christ, they were baptized, both men and women.*

Verses 14-17— *Now when the apostles which were at Jerusalem heard that Samaria had received the word of God, they sent unto them Peter and John: Who, when they were come down, prayed for them, that they might receive the Holy Ghost: (For as yet he was fallen upon none of them: only they were baptized in the name of the Lord Jesus.) Then laid they their hands on them, and they received the Holy Ghost.*

1 Peter 1:23 says that a man is born again *by the word of God, that liveth and abideth for ever.* Acts 8:14 informs us that the Samaritans had received the Word of God. They were born again people. *Later,* Peter and John prayed they would be filled with the Holy Spirit and they were.

What is this work of the Spirit which follows salvation? What is its meaning and purpose?

During His miracle ministry on earth, Jesus said in John 14:10, *The Father that dwelleth in me, he doeth the works.* Verse twelve continues, *He that believeth on me, the works that I do shall he do also; and greater works than these shall he do; because I go unto my Father.* Jesus said that it was the Father dwelling in Him by the Holy Spirit that did the works and miracles in the midst of the people. He also said that those who believed on Him would do those same works (signs, wonders, miracles) and greater works.

How could this be? Acts 1:8 says, *But ye shall receive POWER, after that the Holy Ghost is come upon you: and ye shall be witnesses unto me both in Jerusalem, and in all Judaea, and in Samaria, and unto the uttermost part of the earth.* In Mark chapter sixteen, Jesus commanded His disciples to go forth in the power of the Spirit —*Go ye into all the world, and preach the gospel to every creature* — and signs and wonders would follow them. Verse twenty reads, *And they went forth, and preached everywhere, the Lord working with them, and confirming the word with signs following*. These signs and wonders are evidence and proof that Jesus is still alive today. The born again child of God is to have the Holy Spirit indwelling him to do the works of Jesus. These scriptures speak of the "works" of Jesus, the "power" of the Spirit, and being "witnesses" that Jesus is alive in the earth today. It is the Holy Spirit, dwelling in the heart of the believer, who will do these works and empower the believer to be a witness for Christ.

Notice that in the eighth chapter of Acts, when Peter and John prayed for the Samaritans who had received Christ, they didn't pray that God would *give* them the Holy Ghost. Their prayer was *that they might receive the Holy Ghost* (Acts 8:15). You see, the Holy Spirit came to earth on the day of Pentecost (Acts 2:1,4) and He has been here ever since. How, then, does He come **to dwell** in the heart of the child of God?

The Holy Spirit is a *gift* from God the Father to His children. Your salvation was a free gift. You didn't earn it nor did you deserve it. Eternal life is a free gift. The Holy Spirit is also a free gift from God. Luke 11:9-13 reads, *And I say unto you, ASK, and it shall be given you; seek, and ye shall find; knock, and it shall be opened unto you. For every one that asketh receiveth; and he that seeketh findeth; and to him that knocketh it shall be opened. If a son shall ask bread of any of you that is a father, will he give him a stone? or if he ask a fish, will he for a fish give him a serpent? Or if he shall ask an egg, will he offer him a scorpion? If ye then, being evil, know how to give good gifts unto your children: HOW MUCH MORE shall your heavenly Father give the Holy Spirit to them that ASK Him?*

We see several things from this scripture. If you are a child of God, He has a gift for you and is just waiting for you to ask Him for it. If earthly parents give their children good gifts, HOW MUCH MORE will God give the Holy Spirit to His children who ask! Have no fear about submitting to God in this matter. If you ask for the Holy Spirit, that is exactly what you will receive. God will do what He said He would do.

As it was with salvation, your *will* is the deciding factor. The Father's will is to give you this good gift. But you have the right of *choice* to determine the course of your life. God will not *force* the Holy Spirit on you. You must ask in faith believing that He will do what He says in His Word.

As you receive this gift from God, it is scriptural for you to begin speaking in other tongues. Acts 2:4 says, *And they were all filled with the Holy Ghost, and began to speak with other tongues, as the Spirit gave them utterance.* You will begin to speak in a language that is not known to you. Acts 10:46 says, *For they heard them speak with tongues. . .* Acts 19:6 reads, *And when Paul had laid his hands upon them, the Holy Ghost came on them; and they spake with tongues. . .* Paul said in 1 Corinthians 14:18, *I thank my God, I speak with tongues more than ye all.* 1 Corinthians 14:2 tells us this about tongues, *He that speaketh in an unknown tongue speaketh not unto men, but unto God: for no man understandeth him; howbeit in the spirit he speaketh mysteries.* As the Holy Spirit comes to dwell in your heart, be prepared to speak to God in a language you have not known.

Just as you received Jesus as your Lord by faith, the Holy Spirit is received by faith. God's Word says if you ask, He will give the Spirit to you. You must receive the Spirit and begin to pray in tongues *by faith.* Once you have prayed to receive the Holy Spirit, open your mouth and begin to speak. You speak in

English by moving your tongue and lips and forming words with your mouth. You must do the same things to pray in the Spirit. You have the tongue, the lips, the lungs, and the mouth that will speak. The Holy Spirit will anoint what you speak because you are speaking by faith. As you move out in faith, He will give the utterance. You, however, must make the sounds. English is the voice of your mind, while praying in tongues (in the Spirit) is the voice of your reborn spirit. You can have a supernatural language to help you communicate with God.

There can be hindrances to receiving the Holy Spirit. Involvement in the occult is in direct violation of God's Word. Deuteronomy 18:10-12 reads, *There shall not be found among you any one that useth divination* (fortune telling, ouija boards, automatic writing) ... *or an observer of times* (a person who deals with astrology and horoscopes), *or an enchanter* (magician), *or a witch* (one making contacts with evil spirits), *Or a charmer* (hypnotist), *or a consulter with familiar spirits* (spiritist medium), *or a wizard* (clairvoyant, psychic, ESP, telepathy), *or a necromancer* (one who supposedly communicated with the dead, seances, voodoo). *For all that do these things are an abomination unto the Lord.* Yoga, Transcendental Meditation, Satanism, and other cults all deny that Jesus is the Son of God. The theory of reincarnation directly contradicts the scriptures. Also, a heart with hatred, bitterness, or unforgiveness must be cleansed. You cannot say you love God and at the same time hate your fellow man.

If you have been involved with the occult in any way, or if there has been hatred or bitterness in your heart against anyone, then this must be renounced in order to be filled with God's Spirit. Acts 2:38-39 reads, *Repent, and be baptized every one of you in the name of Jesus Christ for the remission of sins, and ye shall receive the gift of the Holy Ghost. For the promise is unto you, and to*

your children, and to all that are afar off...
This gift is offered to every born again child
of God. The promise of the Holy Spirit as a
gift from God is for YOU. I want you to pray
with me right now to receive the Holy Spirit.
If you will pray with a sincere heart, you will
be filled.

Dear Heavenly Father,
I come to you in the Name of Jesus to
receive the gift of the Holy Spirit. I confess
that Jesus is my Lord and Savior. I now
receive Him as my Baptizer in the Holy
Spirit. I renounce any and all sin in my life.
I repent of any unforgiveness or hatred
and bitterness. I will not hold these in my
heart. I renounce any involvement in the
occult whatsoever. I will not participate in
these ever again. I desire power from on
high that I might do the works of Jesus and
be a witness for Him here on this earth.
You said in Your Word that You will give
the Holy Spirit to those who ask. Father, I
am asking to be filled with the Spirit. Jesus,
baptize me with the Holy Spirit. By faith

in Your Word, I believe that I have received the Holy Spirit. He dwells in my heart. Now, Holy Spirit, as I yield myself to You, pray through me in other tongues.

Now begin to praise and worship God in your new prayer language. Don't speak in English. Phrases and syllables that seem foreign to you will begin to rise up within you. No matter how strange these may sound to you, give voice to them by faith.

John 14:16 (Amplified Bible) says that the Holy Spirit is your *Comforter, Counselor, Helper, Intercessor, Advocate, Strengthener, and Standby.* He will minister to you in each one of these areas. As He dwells in you, He will help you live the Christian life. He will help you get rid of bad habits. Undesirable things in your life will go one by one. The power of God now lives in you so that you can be an OVER-COMER in this life. YOU WILL NEVER BE ALONE AGAIN. The Comforter has come to abide with you forever.

The Bible tells us that God is love. God loves you. In fact, He loved you so much that He sent His Son Jesus to the cross to pay the price for every one of your sins.

The love of God did not stop there. He has sent the Holy Spirit to be with and dwell in those who receive Jesus as their Lord. The Spirit of God is present in the earth today to reveal the Father to His children.

God has given His very best for you. My prayer is that you will determine in your heart to receive His love today.

Dr. Jerry Savelle is a noted author, evangelist, and teacher who travels extensively throughout the United States, Canada, and around the globe. He is president of Jerry Savelle Ministries International, a ministry of many outreaches devoted to meeting the needs of believers all over the world.

Well-known for his balanced Biblical teaching, Dr. Savelle has conducted seminars, crusades and conventions for over twenty-five years and has ministered in thousands of churches and fellowships. He is in great demand today because of his inspiring message of victory and faith and his vivid, and often humorous, illustrations from the Bible. He teaches the uncompromised Word of God with a power and an authority that is exciting, but with a love that delivers the message directly to the spirit man.

In addition to his international headquarters in Crowley, Texas, Dr. Savelle is also founder of JSMI Africa, JSMI United

Kingdom, JSMI South Africa, JSMI Tanzania and JSMI Australia. In 1994, he established the JSMI Bible Institute and School of World Evangelism. It is a two-year school for the preparation of ministers to take the Gospel of Jesus Christ to the nations of the world.

The missions outreach of his ministry extends to over 50 countries around the world. JSMI further ministers the Word of God through its prison ministry outreach.

Dr. Savelle has authored many books and has an extensive video and cassette teaching tape ministry and a nationwide television broadcast. Thousands of books, tapes, and videos are distributed around the world each year through Jerry Savelle Ministries International.

For a complete list of tapes, videos, and
books by Jerry Savelle, write or call:

Jerry Savelle Ministries International
P. 0. Box 748
Crowley, TX 76036
817/297-3155

Feel free to include your prayer requests
and comments when you write.

Other Books by Jerry Savelle:

From Devastation To Restoration

Walking In Divine Favor

Turning Your Dreams Into Reality

Turning Your Adversity Into Victory

Honoring Your Heritage Of Faith

Don't Let Go Of Your Dreams

Faith Building Daily Devotionals

The Force Of Joy

*If Satan Can't Steal Your Joy,
He Can't Keep Your Goods*

A Right Mental Attitude

The Nature Of Faith

The Established Heart

Sharing Jesus Effectively

How To Overcome Financial Famine

You're Somebody Special To God